W9-ANK-010

DISCARD

ISAAC ASIMOV'S NEW LIBRARY OF THE UNIVERSE

DISCOVERING COMETS AND METEORS

BY ISAAC ASIMOV

WITH REVISIONS AND UPDATING BY GREG WALZ-CHOJNACKI

J 523.6
A

Gareth Stevens Publishing
MILWAUKEE

**For a free color catalog describing Gareth Stevens' list of high-quality books,
call 1-800-542-2595 (USA) or 1-800-461-9120 (Canada).
Gareth Stevens' Fax: (414) 225-0377.**

The reproduction rights to all photographs and illustrations in this book are controlled by the
individuals or institutions credited on page 32 and may not be reproduced without their permission.

Library of Congress Cataloging-in-Publication Data

Asimov, Isaac.
  Discovering comets and meteors / by Isaac Asimov; with
revisions and updating by Greg Walz-Chojnacki.
    p. cm. — (Isaac Asimov's New library of the universe)
  Rev. ed. of: Comets and meteors. 1990.
  Includes index.
  Summary: Discusses the characteristics of comets and meteors and
cites both famous appearances and unexplained mysteries connected
with them.
  ISBN 0-8368-1230-1
  1. Comets—Juvenile literature. 2. Meteors—Juvenile literature.
[1. Comets. 2. Meteors.] I. Walz-Chojnacki, 1954-. II. Asimov, Isaac.
Comets and meteors. III. Title. IV. Series: Asimov, Isaac. New library
of the universe.
QB721.5.A832 1996
523.6—dc20   95-40404

This edition first published in 1996 by
Gareth Stevens Publishing
1555 North RiverCenter Drive, Suite 201
Milwaukee, Wisconsin 53212, USA

Revised and updated edition © 1996 by Gareth Stevens, Inc. Original edition published
in 1990 by Gareth Stevens, Inc., under the title *Comets and Meteors*. Text © 1996 by
Nightfall, Inc. End matter and revisions © 1996 by Gareth Stevens, Inc.

All rights to this edition reserved to Gareth Stevens, Inc. No part of this book may be
reproduced, stored in a retrieval system, or transmitted in any form or by any means,
electronic, mechanical, photocopying, recording, or otherwise without the prior
written permission of the publisher except for the inclusion of brief quotations in
an acknowledged review.

Project editor: Barbara J. Behm
Design adaptation: Helene Feider
Editorial assistant: Diane Laska
Production director: Teresa Mahsem
Picture research: Matthew Groshek and Diane Laska

Printed in the United States of America

1 2 3 4 5 6 7 8 9 99 98 97 96

To bring this classic of young people's information up to date, the editors at Gareth
Stevens Publishing have selected two noted science authors, Greg Walz-Chojnacki and
Francis Reddy. Walz-Chojnacki and Reddy coauthored the recent book *Celestial
Delights: The Best Astronomical Events Through 2001.*

Walz-Chojnacki is also the author of the book *Comet: The Story Behind Halley's
Comet* and various articles about the space program. He was an editor of *Odyssey*,
an astronomy and space technology magazine for young people, for eleven years.

Reddy is the author of nine books, including *Halley's Comet*, *Children's Atlas of the
Universe*, *Children's Atlas of Earth Through Time*, and *Children's Atlas of Native
Americans*, plus numerous articles. He was an editor of *Astronomy* magazine for
several years.

CONTENTS

We live in an enormously large place – the Universe. It's just in the last fifty-five years or so that we've found out how large it probably is. It's only natural that we would want to understand the place in which we live, so scientists have developed instruments – such as radio telescopes, satellites, probes, and many more – that have told us far more about the Universe than could possibly be imagined.

We have seen planets up close. We have learned about quasars and pulsars, black holes, and supernovas. We have gathered amazing data about how the Universe may have come into being and how it may end. Nothing could be more astonishing.

Some celestial bodies have been known from very ancient times. Early peoples saw comets in the sky and wondered about them. They were often terrified by them. They also saw "shooting stars," or meteors, and wondered if they were stars that had come loose from the heavens and fallen. How surprised they would have been to learn the truth about comets and meteors that scientific study has provided.

Isaac Asimov

Hazy to Bright

A comet can look like just a hazy patch in the sky. It is made of ice, rock, and gas and appears as a very dim haze at the start. Then it slowly moves among the stars from night to night, getting brighter, then fading again until it disappears.

The hazy patch stretches out into a "tail" that always points away from the direction of the Sun. The tail gets longer as the comet grows brighter, until it sometimes stretches far across the sky. Then the tail shortens and fades.

Ancient peoples imagined a comet as a person's head with long hair streaming behind. In fact, the word *comet* comes from a Greek word meaning "hair."

Opposite: Comet Ikeya-Seki was photographed in the early morning sky near Tucson, Arizona, in 1965.

Left: A woman's head with long hair streaming behind was a favorite image of a comet.

The Oort Cloud and Kuiper Belt

Many comets have been seen throughout human history. In 1950, an astronomer, Jan Oort, had an idea that there must be trillions of comets circling the Sun at a huge distance away. This comet cloud, called the Oort Cloud, consists of icy bodies containing rocky dust.

Comets from the Oort Cloud "fall" toward the Sun when their orbits are disturbed by a passing star or when they collide with each other. Such comets ordinarily travel in orbits around the Sun that take millions of years to complete.

Other comets lie on paths closer to the Sun and take only a few dozen years to complete an orbit. The Kuiper Belt is just such a comet cloud discovered in the 1990s.

Below, left: Like the Oort Cloud, the Kuiper Belt *(shown in gray)* probably holds trillions of comets. Unlike the ball-shaped Oort Cloud, however, the Kuiper Belt comets lie in a flat disk, much like the orbits of the known planets.

Below, right: The Oort Cloud *(shown in red)* circles the Sun at a huge distance away. The larger yellow circle is Pluto's orbit.

Opposite: A rare event in deep space – two comets collide in the Oort Cloud. They may slow down enough to begin the long fall to the Sun, someday appearing in Earth's skies.

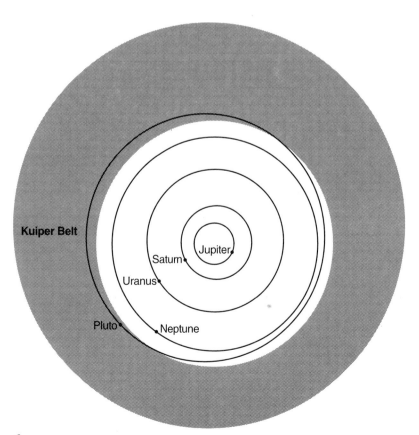

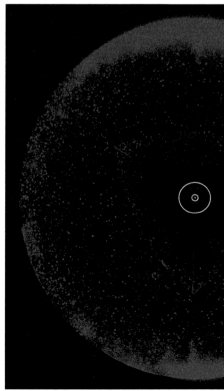

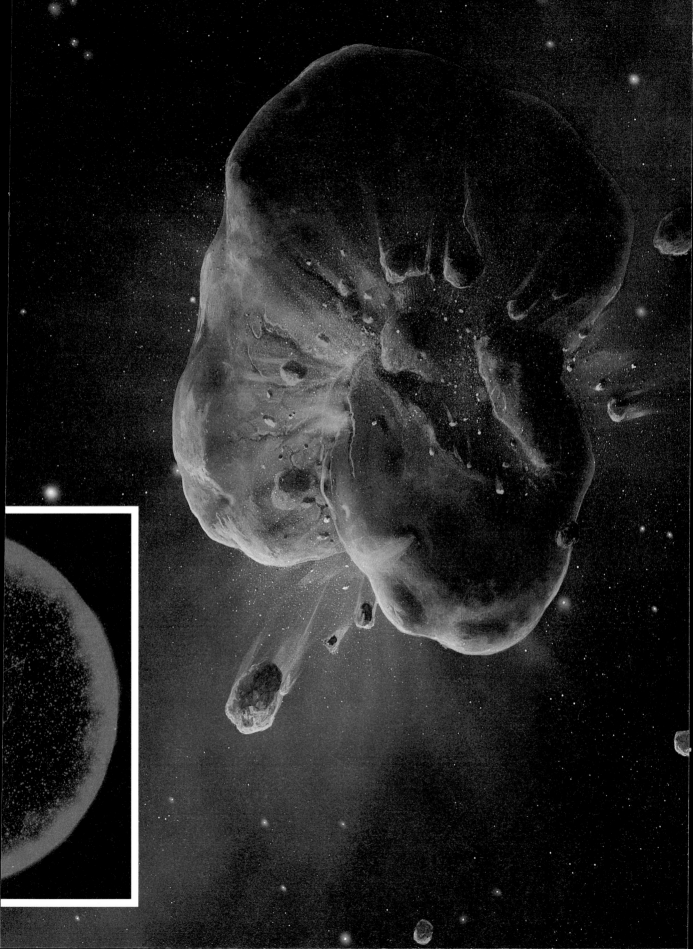

Spectacular Comets

? *What makes a comet flop?*

Sometimes astronomers are fooled into thinking a far-off comet is a large one. Because Comet Kohoutek was seen far off in 1973, it was expected to be a huge, bright comet. It turned out not to be. On the other hand, Comet West, from which little was expected, turned out to be quite bright. Perhaps it is a thick, rocky crust that causes a comet to be duller than expected as it nears the Sun.

Comets come in a variety of sizes and shapes. Some can be quite large. In 1811, a huge comet appeared in the sky. Its head was a cloud of dust that was larger than the Sun, and it had a tail that stretched for millions of miles. The tail consisted entirely of scattered dust.

Other large comets appeared in 1861, in 1882, and in 1910. The comets that appeared in 1861 and in 1910 had tails that appeared to stretch halfway across the sky.

Since 1910, there have been a few bright comets, but none like the spectacular giants before.

Some of history's spectacular comets include:

Donati's Comet in 1858 over Paris, France *(opposite)*; Comet Seki-Lines in 1962 *(inset, opposite)*; and the most famous comet of all, Halley, as it appeared in 1910 *(left)*.

Like Clockwork – Halley's Comet

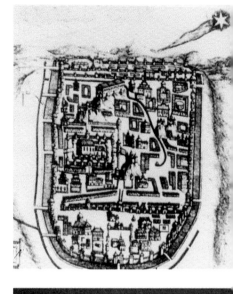

After Sir Isaac Newton developed the Law of Gravity in 1687, his friend Edmund Halley became fascinated with comets. In 1682, a comet had crossed the sky, following the same path as comets in 1531 and 1607.

Using the Law of Gravity, Halley showed that what was thought of as three different comets was actually the same comet traveling around the Sun in a long orbit and returning about every 75-76 years. He predicted the comet would return in 1758 and take its usual path across the sky. In 1759, the comet came back, a year late because Jupiter's strong gravity slowed it down. The comet has since been known as Halley's Comet. It also returned in 1835, 1910, and 1986.

Background: A fifteenth-century drawing of Halley's Comet.

Opposite, top: A sketch from the seventeenth century of Halley's Comet in the skies.

Opposite, bottom: Halley's Comet as it appeared in 1986.

Left: Edmund Halley, the English astronomer who was the first to predict a comet's return.

Below: The *Giotto* space probe took the first close-up pictures of a comet. This picture shows the core of Halley's Comet from 16,155 miles (26,000 kilometers) away.

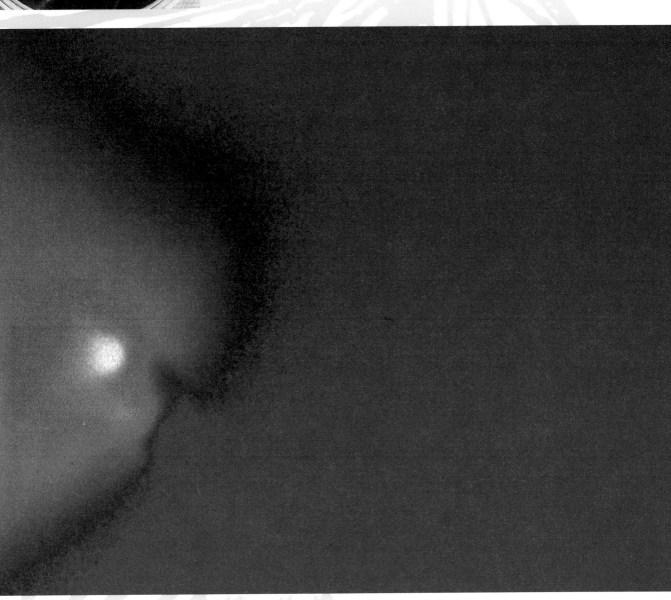

Nothing More Than Dust

Before Halley determined the orbits of comets, people thought comets were a sign of upcoming horrible events on Earth. Because a comet's tail could look like the hair of a wailing woman, or like a sword, people of that time believed comets were predictions of war and disaster.

When a large comet appeared, crowds of people would pray and church bells would ring. Even in fairly recent times, people have panicked over comets. In 1910, it seemed that Earth would pass through the tail of Halley's Comet. Many people were afraid this meant the world would come to an end. But like the tail of every other comet, Halley's tail is dust and nothing more.

Right: In Paris in 1811, many people were afraid that comets would bring disaster.

Inset, top: A humorous and historic look at a grim thought – a comet destroys Earth, while the Man in the Moon smiles on.

Inset, bottom: Montezuma, ruler of the Aztecs, is shown being frightened by a comet in 1520.

? Comets – a prediction of doom?

Halley's Comet appeared in A.D. 66. Four years later, the Jews revolted against Rome and were crushed. Halley's Comet appeared in 1066, and the Saxons of England were defeated by William the Conqueror. It appeared in 1456, and the Turks mopped up the very last bits of the Roman Empire. Whenever any comet appears, there is some sort of war, death, or other disaster. But remember, whenever a comet does not appear, terrible events also occur.

"Shooting Stars" – Meteors

Like comets, meteors have fascinated and frightened people for centuries. Meteors look like stars that shoot across the sky for a distance and then disappear. The word *meteor* comes from the Greek words meaning "things in the air." And, indeed, meteors are shining objects that streak through Earth's atmosphere.

On any clear, moonless night, especially after midnight, such "shooting stars" are visible. Sometimes dozens are visible in a single night. Usually, meteors are quite dim, but sometimes they are bright enough to be called "fireballs."

But meteors are not really stars. The real stars always stay in the sky, no matter how many "shooting stars" streak across the heavens!

? Meteorites – really Moon and Mars rocks?

Some meteorites contain the same materials – and the same proportion of materials – that make up Moon rocks. When meteorites bombarded the Moon and gouged out craters there, the Moon's weak gravity allowed some of the material to be knocked off its surface. Some of the meteorites found on Earth may really be Moon rocks. A very few meteorites include gases with the make-up of the Martian atmosphere, so there may be Mars rocks on Earth, too.

Right: A scientist studies a possible meteorite from Mars that struck the Antarctic.

Opposite: In this illustration, a "fireball" meteor briefly brightens the early morning sky.

Opposite, inset: When a meteor strikes a celestial body, it becomes what is known as a meteorite. Very large meteorites have dug out craters on Earth, the Moon, Mars, and other worlds.

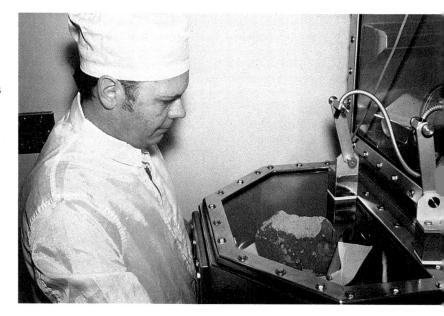

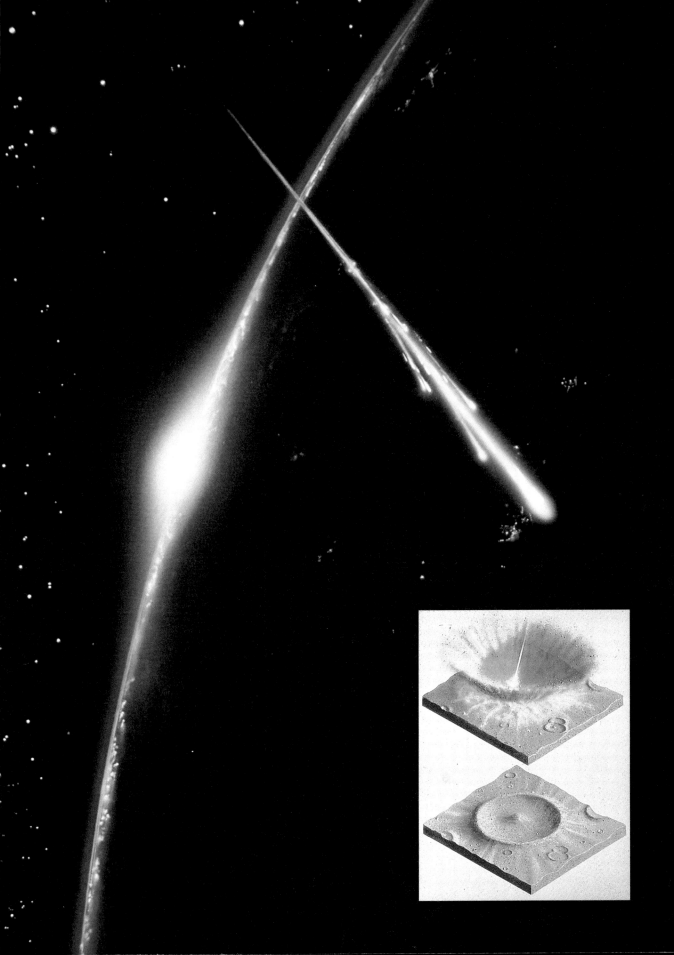

It's Raining Meteors!

Comets and certain kinds of meteors are related. That is because the haze of a comet contains countless particles of dust. This dust drifts away from the comet but continues to orbit the Sun. Over millions of years, the dust spreads along the entire orbit of the comet, and the orbit becomes a band of dust.

Such bands can become quite wide, and Earth actually passes through a few of them each year. When Earth's atmosphere sweeps up the particles, the particles pass rapidly through the air. As a result of friction with the atmosphere, the particles heat up, become white hot, and glow. Observers on Earth see this as a "meteor shower." During such a shower, dozens of meteors can be observed each hour.

Opposite: The remains of a burned-out comet. Tiny dust particles trail along its orbit and eventually become meteors when Earth passes through the dusty path.

Below, left: Comet Bennett, a bright comet that appeared in 1969.

Below, right: A meteor shower occurs when Earth passes through a band of comet dust.

Meteors, Meteoroids, and Meteorites

Not all meteors are caused by comet dust. Many are tiny asteroids or asteroid-like objects made of rock and metal speeding through distant space. While they are in space, meteors are called meteoroids.

Once meteoroids strike Earth's atmosphere and become white hot, they are called meteors. Most meteors are tiny and heat up enough to turn entirely into vapor. But some are large enough that they don't completely burn up. Bits of them survive and strike Earth's surface. These pieces are called meteorites.

Top, left: Over seven thousand meteorites have been found in Antarctica since the 1960s.

Top, right and bottom, left: Comets are like bits of rock and dust mixed into a ball of ice. When the ice ball warms near the Sun, a part of it turns to gas and carries the dust into space.

Opposite, bottom, right: Pictured is a slice through a meteorite. Only the outer crust is affected by its fiery fall to Earth. The rest of the rock provides scientists with clues about the early days of our Solar System.

! Finding meteorites!

Unless you see a meteorite actually fall, you're not likely to find one just by looking on the ground. Most look too much like ordinary rocks. However, in the Arctic and Antarctic regions of Earth, *with their large, remote, ice-covered surfaces, a piece of rock on top of the ice would just about have to be a meteorite. There's really no other way it could have gotten there!*

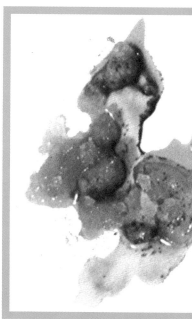

The Sky Is Falling!

Reports of meteor sightings weren't always taken seriously. In 1833, Earth passed through a huge collection of tiny dust particles in space. As many as 200,000 meteors were seen during one night!

It was the biggest meteor shower ever reported. Some people thought it was the end of the world and that all the stars had fallen from the sky. The next night, however, the stars were still there. Reports of the shower got everyone thinking about meteors, and pretty soon it was clear to them that meteors *could* fall from the sky.

Below: The great meteor shower of 1833 is seen from Niagara Falls in this historic drawing.

Right: This illustration shows a unique location for observing a meteor shower – from a balloon!

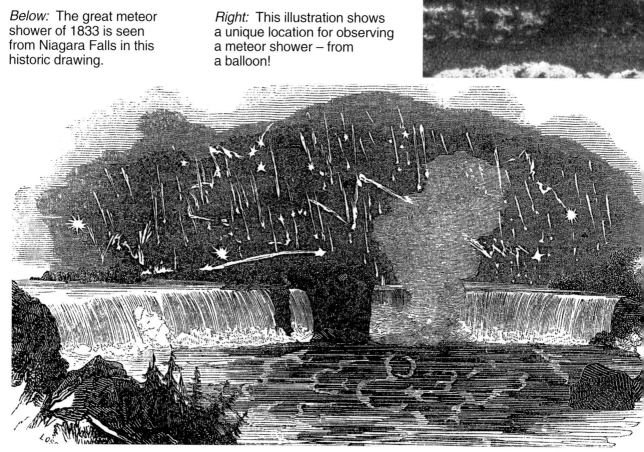

Comets Vanishing

Meteor showers contain material a comet has lost forever. With each trip near the Sun, a comet loses more material. Over the years, the comet shrinks. After a few hundred or thousand orbits, all its icy material is gone.

The rocky core that remains may resemble little more than a small asteroid sailing through the cosmos. If there is no rocky core, the comet vanishes completely and leaves nothing but a cloud of dust.

Occasionally, though, a comet will die in a more spectacular way. In July 1994, a comet crashed into Jupiter, creating some of the most spectacular celestial fireworks ever seen!

? Kamikaze comets?

Some comets fall so near the Sun that they skim only 1 million miles (1.6 million km) or less above its surface. The Sun's heat is enough to break the comets into a string of four or five fragments. These may skim by the Sun on their return visit, like beads on a necklace. Astronomers have even seen comets plunge into the Sun. What makes comets travel so closely to and even crash into the Sun? Scientists do not know for certain.

Right: A comet collides with the Sun in this sequence of photos taken from space in 1979. Comet Howard-Koomen-Michels is shown racing closer to the Sun. Only a cloud of dust and gas emerges from the Sun's other side.

Opposite: Because of the heat of the Sun, this comet's ice is turning to gas and has begun to form a faint tail.

Inset, opposite: In 1994, Comet Shoemaker-Levy 9 was broken into pieces by Jupiter's gravity. It then smashed into the giant planet.

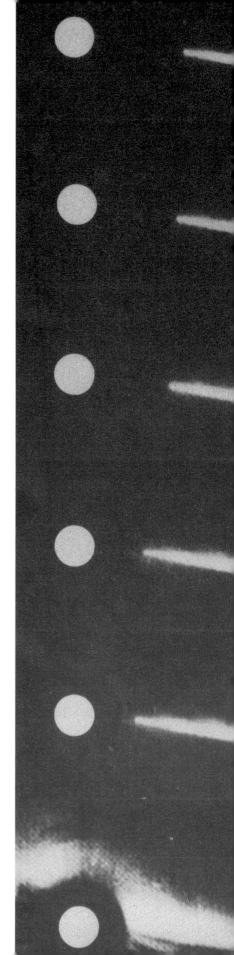

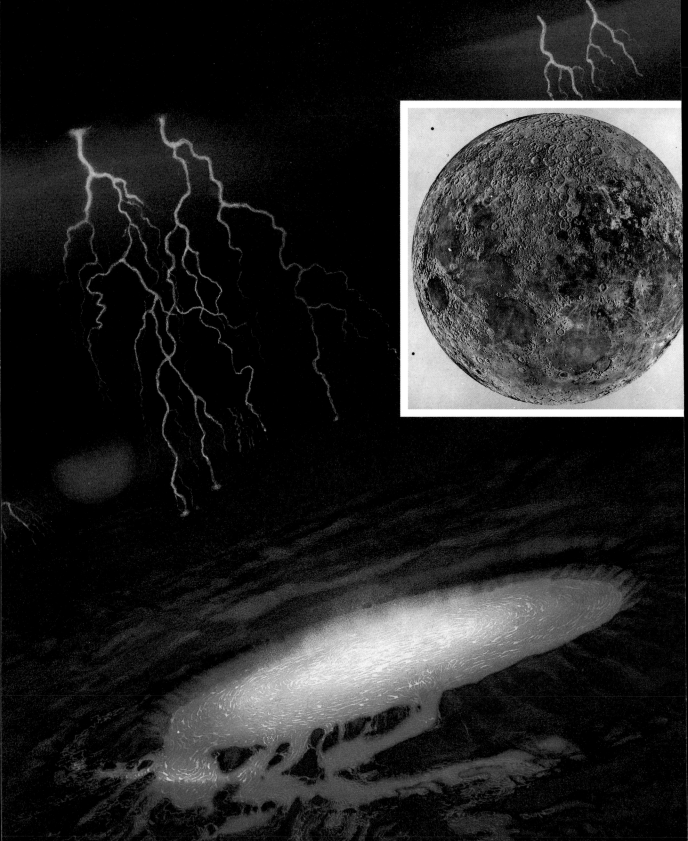

It was 65 million years ago that dinosaurs vanished from Earth. When scientists dig up rocks that are 65 million years old, they find unusual amounts of the rare metal iridium. Such iridium may have come from an object striking Earth. Most scientists now believe that a comet or asteroid strike led to the destruction of the dinosaurs. In the future, could such a strike wipe out other forms of life, including human beings? Hopefully, by then, we will have the technology to predict such an event and take precautions.

Opposite: Both Earth and the Moon were pelted by comets and asteroids shortly after they formed. The atmosphere, oceans, and volcanic activity of our planet erased most of Earth's craters. On the airless Moon *(inset)*, however, the surface has remained mostly unchanged for billions of years.

Visitors from Space

Earth has long been visited by countless objects from space. Most of them burn up harmlessly in our atmosphere as fiery meteors. A few scientists have even suggested that Earth is under daily bombardment by thousands of mini-comets. These mini-comets, over billions of years, would have "flown in" enough water to fill Earth's oceans. Most scientists believe that a comet or asteroid that struck Earth led to the extinction of the dinosaurs.

Sometimes a sizable meteorite or comet hits Earth's surface. There is a crater about 3/4 mile (1.2 km) wide in Arizona where a meteorite may have struck between 15,000 and 40,000 years ago. In 1908, a small comet may have struck in the middle of Siberia, knocking down a forest of trees. If such an impact had taken place on a city, millions of people would have lost their lives.

On Earth, craters formed by such impacts are slowly filled in by the action of wind, water, and volcanoes. On airless worlds, like the Moon, the craters remain intact through time.

Left: Scientists believe they know exactly where a comet or asteroid struck Earth, off the Yucatán Peninsula, that set in motion a chain of events that probably wiped out the dinosaurs.

Cosmic Escapees

Astronomer Charles Kowal discovered what was believed to be an asteroid in 1977 with an orbit that passes between Saturn and Uranus. He named it Chiron. But in 1988, astronomers observed that Chiron has a faintly glowing tail, just like a comet. However, it's much bigger than ordinary comets – perhaps fifty thousand times bigger!

Astronomers now suspect that Chiron is what is known as a centaur that has escaped from the Kuiper Belt. Some scientists even think Pluto and its moon Charon are escapees from the Kuiper Belt.

Below: Chiron (*Ch* in this illustration) is one of six known objects called centaurs *(shown with white orbits)* that may have escaped from the Kuiper Belt. These centaurs give astronomers a good idea of what Kuiper Belt objects are like.

Right: This illustration shows spectacular eruptions on Chiron as it passes Saturn. Chiron orbits the Sun every 50-68 years.

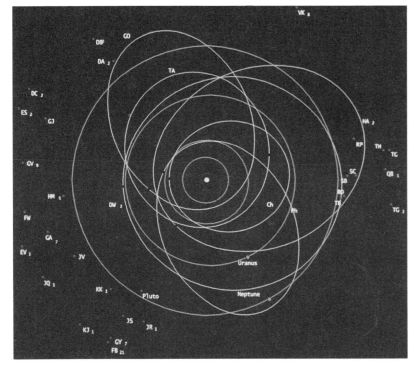

Fact File:
Halley's Comet Through the Ages

Not all ancient peoples were mystified and frightened by comets. For example, the ancient Babylonians suspected that comets were celestial bodies like planets or groups of stars. And by the 1400s to 1500s, European astronomers began treating comets calmly as astronomical phenomena.

In 1682, Edmund Halley had an idea that has affected people's thinking about comets to this very day. He believed that comets travel in elliptical, or oval, paths similar to those of the planets. This meant that comets could be tracked and their Earthly visits calculated and even predicted.

Halley used Newton's Law of Gravity to accurately predict the return of the comet that was eventually named after him. The chart on the next page shows other notable sightings of perhaps the world's favorite and most famous comet – Halley.

Background: Halley's Comet, drawn in Britain, in 1345.

Throughout history, Halley's Comet has been "captured" in various images.

Chinese painting on silk, 168 B.C.

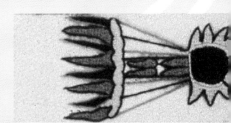

French tapestry, 1066.

Polish illustration, 1600s.

240 B.C. First recorded sighting of Halley's Comet, by Chinese as a "hairy" or "broom" star. After this date, every appearance of Halley on its 75-76 year course has been recorded.

164 B.C. Observation recorded on a Babylonian tablet discovered in 1985.

11 B.C. While the birth of Christ is said to have occurred eleven years later, some historians believe perhaps the birth took place at this time and that the famous Star of Bethlehem may have been Halley's Comet.

A.D. 66 Mentioned in Chinese records. Interpreted as foretelling the destruction of Jerusalem by Rome four years later in A.D. 70.

141-374 This is the time of the Roman Empire, but neither the Romans nor the Greeks are as interested in astronomy as the Chinese, so sightings during this period are mentioned in Chinese records only.

684 The comet is represented in the form of a woodcut in Germany. The comet was supposed to have predicted catastrophic storms, a poor harvest, and plague.

837 Best recorded view to date. Mentioned only in Chinese records. Comes within 5 million miles (8 million km) of Earth. Interpreted to have foretold the death, three years later, of an emperor.

1066 Thought to have foretold the defeat of Harold of England by William the Conqueror of Normandy.

1456 At the request of the pope, Europeans pray against it as an evil omen. Seen as a heavenly comment on the fall of Constantinople to the Turks three years before.

1682 Noted by Edmund Halley, who uses prior sightings and Newton's Law of Gravity to predict the next arrival for 1758.

1759 Halley's first predicted arrival. It is one year later than the original estimate because the comet passes close to the strong gravitational pull of the planet Jupiter.

1835 Thanks in part to astronomers' abilities to predict its arrival, Halley's Comet is enjoyed by many people for the first time. Their fear is replaced by curiosity.

1910 Halley's Comet is examined scientifically and considered not dangerous to beings on Earth. Even so, people buy special pills as protection against the imagined poisonous effects of the comet. At this sighting, the tail stretches across the sky.

1986 In some ways, this was the most disappointing sighting in two thousand years. The comet spent its brightest time farthest away from Earth, so our view of Halley was faint when it reached its closest distance to Earth on April 10. But thanks to modern methods of gathering information, including the rocket probes sent from Earth to meet Halley, astronomers gathered exciting information about Halley and comets in general. This was also an important sighting in other ways because it involved international scientific cooperation.

Italian painting by Giotto, 1300s.

Photograph, 1910.

Computer-generated image, 1986.

29

More Books about Comets and Meteors

Asimov's Guide to Halley's Comet. Asimov (Walker)
Comet. Sagan (Random House)
Comet: The Story Behind Halley's Comet. Walz-Chojnacki (AstroMedia/Gareth Stevens)
Comets, Asteroids, and Meteors. Fradin (Childrens Press)
Comets and Meteors. Couper (Franklin Watts)
Cosmic Debris: The Asteroids. Asimov (Gareth Stevens)
Death from Space: What Killed the Dinosaurs? Asimov (Gareth Stevens)
How Did We Find Out About Comets? Asimov (Avon)

Videos

The Asteroids. (Gareth Stevens)
Comets and Meteors. (Gareth Stevens)

Places to Visit

You can explore the Universe – including places where comets and meteors roam – without leaving Earth. Here are some museums and centers where you can find a variety of space exhibits.

The Space and Rocket Center
    and Space Camp
One Tranquility Base
Huntsville, AL 35807

International Women's Air and
    Space Museum
One Chamber Plaza
Dayton, OH 45402

Anglo-Australian Observatory
Private Bag
Coonarbariban 2357 Australia

Astrocentre
Royal Ontario Museum
100 Queen's Park
Toronto, Ontario M5S 2C6

San Diego Aero-Space Museum
2001 Pan American Plaza
Balboa Park
San Diego, CA 92101

Ontario Science Centre
770 Don Mills Road
Don Mills, Ontario M3C 1T3

Places to Write

Here are some places you can write for more information about comets and meteors. Be sure to state what kind of information you would like. Include your full name and address for a reply.

NASA Lewis Research Center
Educational Services Office
21000 Brookpark Road
Cleveland, OH 44135

Canadian Space Agency
Communications Department
6767 Route de L'Aeroport
Saint Hubert, Quebec J3Y 8Y9

Jet Propulsion Laboratory
Teacher Resource Center
4800 Oak Grove Drive
Pasadena, CA 91109

Sydney Observatory
P. O. Box K346
Haymarket 2000 Australia

Glossary

asteroid: very small planets made of rock or metal. There are thousands of them in our Solar System, and they orbit the Sun in large numbers between Mars and Jupiter. But some appear elsewhere in the Solar System – some as meteoroids and some possibly as "captured" moons of planets, such as Mars.

astronomer: a person involved in the scientific study of the Universe and its various celestial bodies.

atmosphere: the gases that surround a planet, star, or moon.

billion: the number represented by 1 followed by nine zeroes – 1,000,000,000. In some countries, this number is called "a thousand million." In these countries, one billion would then be represented by 1 followed by twelve zeroes – 1,000,000,000,000 – a million million.

centaurs: asteroid-like objects in space that may have escaped from the Kuiper Belt.

comet: an object in space made of ice, rock, and gas. It has a vapor tail that may be seen when the comet's orbit brings it close to the Sun.

crater: a hole or pit on a planet or moon created by volcanic explosions or the impact of meteorites.

evaporation: the process that turns water into a vapor or gas.

fireballs: meteors that enter Earth's atmosphere in a bright and spectacular manner.

gravity: the force that causes objects like Earth and the Moon to be drawn to one another.

Halley's Comet: the comet that passes Earth every 75-76 years. It was named for Edmund Halley, the English astronomer. Every visit by this comet has been documented since its first definite recorded sighting by the Chinese in 240 B.C. Its last pass of Earth occurred in 1986.

meteor: a meteoroid that has entered Earth's atmosphere. Also, the bright streak of light made as the meteoroid enters or moves through the atmosphere.

meteor shower: a concentrated group of meteors, visible when the Earth's orbit intersects debris from a comet.

meteorite: a meteoroid when it strikes Earth.

meteoroid: a lump of rock or metal drifting through distant space. Meteoroids can be as big as asteroids or as small as specks of dust.

orbit: the path that one celestial object follows as it circles, or revolves, around another.

probe: a craft that travels in space, photographing and gathering data about celestial bodies, and even landing on some of them.

"shooting star": a meteor that appears as a temporary streak of light in the night sky.

star: mainly gaseous material, massive enough to initiate (or to have once initiated) nuclear reactions in its central regions.

Sun: Earth's star and provider of the energy that makes life on our planet possible.

vapor: a gas formed from a solid or liquid. On Earth, clouds are made from water vapor.

Index

Born in 1920, Isaac Asimov came to the United States as a young boy from his native Russia. As a young man, he was a student of biochemistry. In time, he became one of the most productive writers the world has ever known. His books cover a spectrum of topics, including science, history, language theory, fantasy, and science fiction. His brilliant imagination gained him the respect and admiration of adults and children alike. Sadly, Isaac Asimov died shortly after the publication of the first edition of *Isaac Asimov's Library of the Universe.*

The publishers wish to thank the following for permission to reproduce copyright material: front cover, © Paul Dimare; 4, © Dennis Milon; 4-5, © Keith Ward 1989; 6, © Gareth Stevens, Inc.; 6-7, © Julian Baum 1988; 7, © Mark Maxwell 1989; 8 (large), Mary Evans Picture Library; 8 (inset), © Alan McClure; 8-9, Yerkes Observatory; 10 (upper), Jet Propulsion Laboratory, International Halley Watch; 10 (lower), Courtesy Harold Reitsema, Ball Aerospace Systems Division/© 1986 Max Planck Institute; 10-11 (background), © Gareth Stevens, Inc., 1989; 10-11, Max Planck Institute, West Germany; 11, Jet Propulsion Laboratory, International Halley Watch; 12-13 (inset), Neg. #282680, Courtesy Department of Library Services, American Museum of Natural History; 12-13 (large), Mary Evans Picture Library; 13, © Gareth Stevens, Inc., 1989; 14, NASA; 15 (large), © Mark Paternostro; 15 (inset), © Garret Moore 1987; 16, © Michael Carroll; 16-17, © Helen and Richard Lines; 17, © Keith Ward 1989; 18-19 (upper), © Edward J. Olsen; 18-19 (lower), 19 (upper), Matthew Groshek/© Gareth Stevens, Inc., 1989; 19 (lower), © Edward J. Olsen; 20, Historical Pictures Service, Chicago; 20-21, Mary Evans Picture Library; 22, Naval Research Laboratory; 23 (large), © Paul Dimare 1987; 23 (inset), Jet Propulsion Laboratory; 24 (large), © Bruce Bond; 24 (inset), U. S. Geological Survey, courtesy of Don E. Wilhelms and Donald E. Davis; 25, © Joe Tucciarone 1987; 26, Courtesy Minor Planet Center; 26-27, © William K. Hartmann; 28 (all), 29 (upper and center), © Anne Norcia 1985; 29 (lower), NASA.

DISCARD

J
523.6   Asimov, Isaac.
A
         Discovering comets and
         meteors.

Hiram Halle Memorial Library
Pound Ridge, New York

GAYLORD